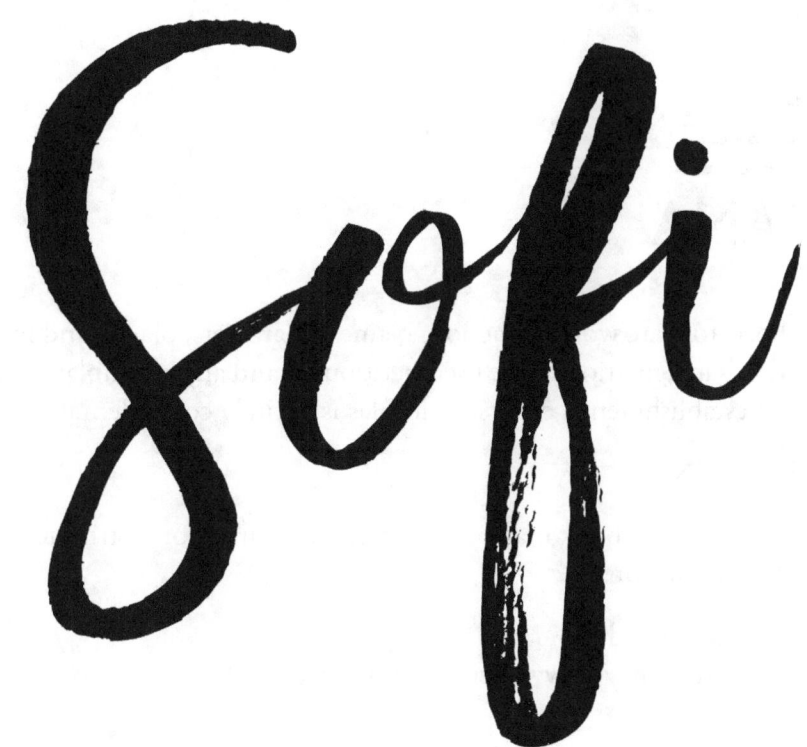

# Sofi

A SCREENPLAY BY
NATHAN NIX

**Sofi: A Screenplay by Nathan Nix**
Written by Nathan Nix
All-Americana Publishing

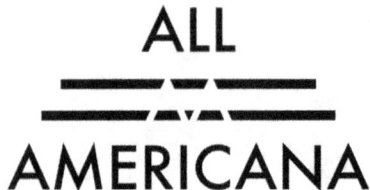

Cover design by Steven Bedingfield
Cover painting by Meredith Richey (www.meredithricheyart.com)
Author photo by Dave Mackie

# A NOTE FROM THE AUTHOR

While writing my first Young Adult novel, *The Drifters*, in 2013, I toyed with the idea of continuing the tales of my main characters in an ongoing episodic series of online short stories. They would pick up about 10 years after the book and chronicle the lives of Ryan, Sofi and Nic as thirtysomethings in Houston and its surrounding suburbs. A few of these got written before marketing the book took over my life and caused me to get distracted.

Fast-forward a few years. With my interest in filmmaking revived after a decade since my first foray into movies, I was on the search for a story to turn into a short film. Of the many ideas I revisited, one of the few short stories that did get written stuck out as a real contender. It was called *Everybody Reproduces* and followed Ryan and Sofi, two thirtysomething artists living in Houston, as they returned to the suburbs of their youth for a friend's baby shower. Over the course of an afternoon, amidst awkward baby shower games and even more awkward encounters with old friends (some more welcome than others), they were forced to examine whether they were truly happy with the people they'd become and the direction they were headed.

Having recently returned from Nashville to the North Houston suburb of my youth, *Everybody Reproduces* resonated strongly with me. I decided it was perfect for the short film. Not only was it a funny, simple story that could be told in minimal locations for a low budget, but it was also *about* something — what are we willing to sacrifice for our dreams?

I was at a crossroads myself. Was it time to give up the dream of writing screenplays and making films and take a well-paying job with great benefits that I wasn't passionate about? Was I tired of striving for something I may never achieve? All my friends were getting married, buying houses and having kids. They were investing in things that seemed to have lasting value, but many were laying down the dreams of their youth in exchange for these things. Did they have it right? What if I sacrificed all of those things and achieved my dreams only to discover that they held a hollow promise? Would it still have been worth it?

These are the things Sofi weighs in this script. In the end, she doesn't have the answer, and neither do I. The answer is probably different for everyone anyway. You have to balance your gut feelings with as much wisdom as you can absorb.

I am forever indebted to you for donating to help me bring this script to life. I hope you feel your investment in me and this community of artists was a wise decision. This script and short story are just a small token of our appreciation for your generosity.

EXT. HOUSTON - DAY

Shots of various parts of Houston:

* Greetings from Houston sign in The Heights

* The downtown skyline

* A quinceañera group jumps for a photo at the Color Wall

* Leopard Lounge in Montrose


EXT. HIGH SCHOOL FOR THE PERFORMING AND VISUAL ARTS

SOFI (30s), a hipster teacher dressed in all black, leaves
work for the day and heads out into Montrose.


EXT. HOUSTON - DAY

Sofi walks through Montrose on her way to the bar. The
neighborhood around her is alive -- cyclists, people smoking
cigarettes on stoops, and homeless wandering the street.


EXT. POISON GIRL - DAY

Sofi enters the neighborhood dive bar.


INT. POISON GIRL - DAY

Sofi is sitting alone at a table and sketching, a glass of
wine next to her.

Across the bar, a GUY READING A BOOK steals a look her way.
She doesn't notice. He steals another, obviously interested
in her, but she catches him this time. He looks at the book,
embarrassed to have been caught. Sofi grins.

The guy rises and walks Sofi's direction, apparently having
made up his mind to talk to her.

Sofi senses him coming and casts him a quick, inviting
glance. As he approaches, her CELL PHONE goes off and an
OBNOXIOUS RINGTONE assaults the bar.

Sofi GASPS and grabs the phone to silence it.

The guy has a split-second to decide whether or not to
continue towards her. He bails on the encounter and heads to
the restroom, confused and disappointed.

Sofi holds the phone. She's also confused and disappointed. She finally looks at who's calling.

INSERT PHONE

The Caller ID says "NIC" and features a picture of a woman in her late 20s wearing a multicolored wig at a party.

BACK TO SCENE

Sofi is sort of stunned. She starts to answer it and then stops. She hesitates as she considers what to do. Eventually she sets the phone down and the call ends.

Sofi is disappointed in herself. She knows she should've answered. She starts to sketch again, but it's on her mind.

BEEP! The phone lets her know a voicemail has been left.

                    SOFI
              (frustrated)
          Who leaves a voicemail?


EXT. POISON GIRL BACK PATIO - DAY

Sofi exits the back door and listens to the voicemail.

                    NIC (O.S.)
              (on phone)
          Hey, it's me, and yes, I'm leaving
          you a voicemail. Did you get the
          invite to this couples baby shower
          they're throwing for me? You didn't
          RSVP, which I know is because of
          this fear of commitment thing you
          swear you don't have, but I
          really want you there, so I'm not
          gonna stop calling until you agree
          to come. I promise you'll know
          people. And there'll be wine. Mel's
          putting this thing on, and while I
          love her to death, I need you to
          help keep me sane. Plus we haven't
          got to hang since you moved back. I
          know you hate coming back home to
          the 'burbs, but I wanna see you, so
          please come. Bye.

                    SOFI
              (feeling guilty)
          Aw, man.

                                        FADE TO BLACK:

**SUPERIMPOSE TITLE: SOFI**


INT. SOFI'S APARTMENT - DAY

Sofi searches through her clothes for the right outfit. She holds a couple of brightly colored options up and even tries different headwear with it. Nothing works. She finally settles on what she's already wearing: a black blouse and purple jeans.


EXT. SOFI'S CAR - DAY

Sofi's car pulls away as she heads out.


INT. SOFI'S CAR - DAY

Sofi applies makeup as she navigates the roads.


EXT. SUBURBAN NEIGHBORHOOD - DAY

As Sofi drives, she looks out her window at suburban scenes:

* "The Woodlands" sign and deer statues

* American flags on houses

* Kids playing basketball in a driveway

She sees a MOM PUSHING A STROLLER on the sidewalk, a LITTLE GIRL following behind and playing on an iPhone.

The mom looks at Sofi and gives her a wave. The little girl looks up from her iPhone and gives Sofi a death stare.


EXT. SUBURBAN HOUSE - DAY

Sofi's car pulls to a stop in the driveway of a suburban house. A few cars are already there. A SIGN with a balloon attached announces that a baby shower is taking place inside.

Sofi exits the car and looks around. She takes a breath and walks to the door.


EXT. SUBURBAN HOUSE - LATER

Sofi hesitates at the door. A SMALL, WRAPPED PRESENT is in her hands. LAUGHTER and VOICES filter through the door.

Sofi leans forward to hear. She's contemplating not going in but eventually summons the courage and pushes the door open.


INT. SUBURBAN HOUSE - CONTINUOUS

Sofi enters cautiously and scopes the place out. PARTY PEOPLE CHAT in the background.

                    NIC (O.S.)
               (calling out)
          Sofi!

Nic from the iPhone Caller ID, now a cheerful, pregnant, clean-cut woman, approaches Sofi, who is relieved to see her.

                    SOFI
          Hey, you!

They hug like the long-lost friends they are.

                    NIC
          Oh my God! I'm so glad you came. I
          didn't know if you would.

                    SOFI
          What? Of course I came. I'm not
          gonna miss this. Look at you --
          you're pregnant!

Nic laughs.

                    SOFI (CONT'D)
          There's, like, an entire person
          developing limbs and consciousness
          inside you.

                    NIC
          Right?

                    SOFI
          That's...so weird.

                    NIC
          I know!
               (re: the present)
          Here, let me take that. I'll put it
          with the others.
               (taking it, teasing)
          Oh, it's light! Like super light.
          What is it?

                    SOFI
          You'll have to wait and see.

                    NIC
          Oh, I can't wait. You always give
          the best gifts.
                    (pulling her towards the
                    living room)
          Come say hi to the girls.

She leads Sofi towards the living room.

                    SOFI (O.C.)
          Hey, you said something about
          wine...


INT. SUBURBAN HOUSE - LATER

Sofi with LANA (late 20s), a polite, unassuming suburban mom
who talks fast and is eager to impress.

                    LANA
          We were all coming up with new
          mommy tips for Nic earlier. Do you
          have anything to share?

                    SOFI
          Well, I don't have any kids, so
          I've got nothing to contribute.

                    LANA
                    (eager for any info)
          No kids? Oh. Do you want any?

                    SOFI
          Why, you got some you're trying to
          move along?

Lana laughs too hard. Sofi gets a kick out of this.

                    SOFI (CONT'D)
                    (pretend calling out)
          Uh-oh, we got a child trafficker
          here! Call the police!

Lana sobers quickly, a bit worried.

                    LANA
          Oh please don't joke about that.
          There's a lawyer lady from my
          church who helps free child slaves
          in India, and she says it's
          terrible, just terrible.

                    SOFI
                (stunned)
          Wow. No, you're right. I didn't--

                    LANA
                (interrupting, cheery
                 again)
          So are you seeing anybody?

Sofi is speechless at Lana's quick recovery.

                                        CUT TO:

Sofi pours wine. Takes a sip. Fills more. Turns to leave.

                    MEL (O.S.)
          You teach art in the city, right?

Surprised, Sofi finds MEL (late 20s), a Queen Bee turned
immaculate suburban saleswoman, looming over her.

                    SOFI
          Holy...! Jeez, Mel.
                (recovering)
          Um, yeah I do. How'd you know that?

                    MEL
          Facebook.

                    SOFI
                (without thinking)
          We're Facebook friends?

Mel misses the comment and starts into a pitch.

                    MEL
          You know, I was teaching too until
          I became a mommy. But then I found
          a career that let me stay at home
          with my babies but still be able to
          help others, which is really my
          passion. It's so fulfilling.

                    SOFI
                (hesitant)
          Oh yeah?

                    MEL
          It's the most incredible story. It
          all starts with a life-changing
          product called Plexus Slim.

                                        CUT TO:

Sofi shows Lana PHOTOS OF PAINTINGS on her phone.

                    LANA
I <u>love</u> them. But your paintings
don't have any faces.

                    SOFI
Well, I'm painting memories, and
often we remember things sort of
hazily, without fully realized
settings or, you know, faces. But
then we have to navigate between
our memories and reality...

Lana tries to comprehend...

                    SOFI (CONT'D)
So I'm trying to acknowledge the
contradiction between these faded
pasts and...
       (realizing Lana's lost,
        giving up)
...these real, disjointed
experiences.

                    LANA
       (not getting it)
I <u>totally</u> get it.

                    SOFI
       (disbelieving)
Really?

                    LANA
       (proud)
Sofi, I know you haven't seen me in
awhile, but I'm <u>so</u> different than I
was in high school. I voted for
Obama, if you can believe that.
       (beat)
Well, the first time.

                              CUT TO:

Mel still has Sofi cornered and is in full-on pitch mode,
completely oblivious to anything Sofi might be saying.

                    MEL
I mean, I was almost three hundred
pounds. Imagine that!

                    SOFI
Oh, I'm trying.

                         MEL
          And look at me now! I don't want to
          toot my own horn, but I'm kind of
          MILF-y, right? Sofi, Plexus Slim
          literally changed my entire life.
          And it can do the same for you.

                         SOFI
          Oh, I didn't realize I needed--

Mel realizes she might've gone too far and backpedals.

                         MEL
          No, I'm not saying you <u>need</u> to,
          just that if you want to, you know,
          trim up a bit in...
               (looking her up and down)
          ...places. Not that you need to.
          Just if you want to. But not that
          you need to.

Beat.

          MEL (CONT'D)                         SOFI
     If you want to.              If I want to.

                         SOFI
          Got it.


INT. SUBURBAN HOUSE - LATER

Sofi stands in the dining room by herself, a near-empty glass
of wine in hand as she checks out the host's decor.

                         NIC (O.S.)
          Are you hiding?

Sofi looks over to see Nic holding a glass of wine.

                         NIC (CONT'D)
          I got you more.

Sofi smiles.


INT. SUBURBAN HOUSE - LATER

Sofi and Nic sit at a dining table talking.

                         NIC
          Mel give you her Plexus spiel?

Sofi takes a big swig of wine in response.

>                     NIC (CONT'D)
>          That's a yes. You sign up?

Sofi gives her a look.

>                     NIC (CONT'D)
>          Good. 'Cause if you're gonna be in
>          anyone's downline, it's mine.

>                     SOFI
>               (shocked)
>          Nicole!

>                     NIC
>               (embarrassed)
>          Don't judge me! You only had to
>          endure it for ten minutes. She was
>          after me for a month. I caved! It's
>          not like it isn't effective -- she
>          did lose weight...

>                     SOFI
>          No, it's that you're basically
>          working for her, right? I can't
>          even imagine...

>                     NIC
>          Oh, it can be freaking brutal --
>          like if they remade Glengarry Glen
>          Ross with Martha Stewart: "Pumpkin
>          spice lattes are for closers!"

They laugh.

>                     SOFI
>          I freaking miss you, dude.

>                     NIC
>          Me too! How have we not seen each
>          other since you moved back? I mean,
>          we haven't even unpacked your whole
>          New York experience.

>                     SOFI
>          Yeah, New York. Jeez.

>                     NIC
>          Sorry it didn't work out.

>                     SOFI
>          It's fine. It was a wake-up call,
>          you know? Like a reality check.

                    NIC
          No way. You just need to find your
          audience. Like suburban moms.

Sofi laughs hard.

                    NIC (CONT'D)
          They love your work!

                    SOFI
          Lana had no idea what I was talking
          about when I explained it.

                    NIC
          Lana never has any idea what anyone
          is talking about. But I bet she's
          still gonna buy a piece. I'm just
          saying -- if you're looking for
          something different, the house next
          door is for rent.

                    SOFI
          You're out of control. I couldn't
          afford to live up here even if I
          wanted to.

                    NIC
          Well, not by yourself you can't...

                    SOFI
          Oh my God.

                    NIC
          I just worry about you in town all
          alone. What if you get the flu and
          try to take care of yourself and
          fail? And then you're lying on the
          floor, incapacitated, and you can't
          reach the telephone. And then you
          die. All because I moved back to
          the 'burbs.
               (beat)
          Tell me you'll think about it.

                    SOFI
          I love you and I'm happy that
          you're happy, but there's nothing
          for me up here. Sorry.

Mel appears behind them.

                    MEL
               (stoked)
          Ladies, it's game time!

                        NIC
          Ok, we're coming.

Mel leaves.

                        SOFI
          She's still fun.


INT. SUBURBAN HOUSE - LATER

Sofi reloads on snacks in the kitchen as the group gathers in
the living room for games. Suddenly...

                        NIC (O.S.)
                    (shocked)
          Oh my god -- Ryan!

Sofi's head shoots up at the name, fear in her eyes.

A new guest -- RYAN (30s) who was once probably cool and in a
band -- has arrived. He hugs Nic.

                        NIC (CONT'D)
          I didn't think you were coming.

                        RYAN
          I wouldn't miss it.

Sofi is petrified.

As Ryan hugs Nic, his back still to Sofi, Nic mouths to Sofi:
"I'm so sorry!" and "Please don't leave."

Sofi eyes an escape route through the kitchen, the FRONT DOOR
just beyond it.

Ryan and Nic separate, and Nic can't help but shoot a quick
glance Sofi's way.

Ryan turns and sees Sofi. Both are too stunned to say
anything. Sofi can't run away now. She forces a smile and
offers a pathetic wave.

She gathers herself and heads into the living room. Nervous,
he moves to hug her.

                        RYAN (CONT'D)
          Hi.

                        SOFI
          Hey you.

They share a brief, awkward hug and quickly separate.

                    RYAN
          How are you?

                    SOFI
          Good. And you?

                    RYAN
          Great. It's good to see you.

                    SOFI
          Yeah...ditto.

                    RYAN
          How was New York?

                    SOFI
               (slight hesitation)
          Great. Amazing.

He caught the hesitation and his interest is piqued.

                    RYAN
          But now you're back.

                    SOFI
          Yeah.
               (quickly changing the
                subject)
          How about you? How's...life?

                    RYAN
          Life? Um...good? Where to start?
          Well, I bought a house. I'm a home
          owner now.

                    SOFI
          Wow. Congratulations. How very
          adult of you.

                    RYAN
          I know, right? Figured it was about
          time. Everybody else our age has
          got houses and kids and dogs
          and...lawn equipment.

                    SOFI
          Ha! Right? I know owning a quality
          mulcher was always your dream.
          Where'd you buy?

                    RYAN
          Around the corner actually. Got it
          a couple months ago.

                    SOFI
              (genuinely surprised)
        Wait, you moved out of the city?

                    RYAN
        You seem super surprised.

                    SOFI
        I just... What about your music?

                    RYAN
              (laughing)
        My music? It didn't seem like it
        was going anywhere, so I sold most
        of my gear and put a down payment
        on the house.

This change starts Sofi's wheels turning, reassessing...

                    RYAN (CONT'D)
        Just kept my acoustic guitar to,
        you know, like, teach my kid one
        day, pass it on.
              (off her look)
        Future kid. Theoretical kid.
              (super awkward)
        I'm single at the moment.

The IMMENSE AWKWARDNESS between them is pierced by...Mel
CLAPPING her hands to bring things to order. She addresses
them as if one of her old 1st grade classes.

                    MEL
        All right, everyone -- if I can
        have your attention... All eyes up
        here, please.
              (satisfied)
        Welcome to Nicole's baby shower!
        I'm so glad you could make it.
        We're going to have so much fun
        today eating food, playing games
        and opening presents for
        little...well, we don't know her
        name because Nic is keeping it to
        herself until that little miracle
        hanging out in her belly makes her
        first appearance.

Sofi instinctively turns to Ryan to say something, hesitates,
and then decides against it.

Ryan saw Sofi. He considers her for a moment.

                    MEL (CONT'D)
          Ok, grab your partner and, in the
          words of the goddess Fergie...
                    (singing)
          *Let's get it started in here!*

The entire room slowly rises except Sofi and Ryan. As Mel
gets on to Lana in the background, it hits Sofi and Ryan that
everyone else is paired up.

                    MEL (CONT'D)
          Lana, that was the cue! Where's the
          freaking song? We talked about
          this.

Sofi raises her hand for Mel to see.

                    MEL (CONT'D)
          Question?

                    SOFI
          Do you have to have a partner?

                    MEL
          Well <u>yeah</u>, of course.

                    SOFI
          Of course.

Ryan and Sofi sheepishly look at each other.

                    RYAN
          Guess it's you and me.

                    SOFI
          Let's do it.


INT. SUBURBAN HOUSE - LATER

Every man is blindfolded while the women feed them baby food.
It's <u>loud</u> as the guys shout out their guesses of what flavor
they're tasting. Sofi feeds Ryan.

                    RYAN
          Pears, I think...um, hints of
          corn...and something else.

                    SOFI
                    (whispering)
          Zucchini.

                    RYAN
                (surprised)
            Zucchini?

                    SOFI
            Yes!

                    MEL
            No cheating, no cheating!

                    RYAN
            Who gives a baby zucchini?

Sofi, into the game, sticks the next flavor into his mouth.

                    SOFI
            Shut up and taste!


INT. SUBURBAN HOUSE - LATER

The couples hold baby bottles filled with beer.

                    MEL
                Go!

All chug. Ryan is going slower than everyone else.

                    SOFI
            Come on, dude! Chug!

He struggles.

                    SOFI (CONT'D)
            What are you doing to that nipple?
                (beat)
            Oh, I remember that.

His eyes FLASH wide in embarrassment.

                    SOFI (CONT'D)
                (turning away)
            I can't even watch this.

Another couple finishes first. Sofi throws her hands up in
exasperation. Ryan is still chugging.

                    SOFI (CONT'D)
                (slaps him in the belly)
            Dude!

He nearly spews the beer.

INT. SUBURBAN HOUSE - LATER

Each couple swaddles a stuffed animal. Sofi struggles.

> RYAN
> Do you want me to--

> SOFI
> (frustrated)
> No, I got it!

But she doesn't have it.

> RYAN
> Here, just...

He moves closer to her -- up against her -- and GRAZES HER HAND as he smiles and takes over.

Warning bells go off in Sofi's head as she gives him space to swaddle (which he does like a total pro).

She looks at every other couple in the room, each spouse huddled close as they work as a team. Sofi watches Ryan...considers him...

> RYAN (CONT'D)
> Done!

He raises his arms in triumph and she snaps out of it. He turns, stoked, and gives her a HIGH FIVE.

INT. SUBURBAN HOUSE - LATER

All the guys hold a tennis ball as Mel explains the rules.

> MEL
> So you're going to take the ball
> and place it on your forehead.

The guys do.

> MEL (CONT'D)
> Turn and face your lady.

They obey. Ryan, feeling goofy, smiles. Sofi returns the smile but quickly looks back to Mel.

> MEL (CONT'D)
> Ladies, press your forehead to the
> other side of the ball.

They do so. Sofi hesitates as she realizes just how close she's going to have to get to Ryan. She reluctantly obeys though. They're eye-to-eye, inches away.

It's the first time they've looked each other in the eye and held each other's gaze since they broke up.

                    MEL (CONT'D)
          I'm going to read out a list of
          moves you have to make as a couple.

They continue looking each other in the eye. Ryan is almost giddy, but Sofi grows extremely unnerved.


INT. RYAN AND SOFI'S APARTMENT - NIGHT [FLASHBACK]

Sofi and Ryan sit opposite each other, cross-legged, on their bed. They stare at something small in Sofi's hands.

A PREGNANCY TEST. She shakes it, but no result yet.

Ryan is excited, anxious. Sofi is filled with worry, dread.

She looks up from the unresponsive pregnancy test and looks him in the eyes, searching them for something reassuring.

                                        BACK TO:


INT. SUBURBAN HOUSE - DAY

Current-day Ryan and Sofi look each other in the eyes. The same looks appear on their faces: his hopeful, hers unsure.

                    MEL
          Take one big step to your right.

Everyone obeys. A couple of people drop their tennis balls.

                    MEL (CONT'D)
               (to them)
          You're out!

Sofi and Ryan succeed.

                    MEL (CONT'D)
          Jump.

Many fail, but Sofi and Ryan succeed. He's stoked, which doesn't set her at ease. Mel clears the losers out so the remaining three couples have room for the next challenge.

INT. RYAN AND SOFI'S APARTMENT - NIGHT [FLASHBACK]

They wait on the pregnancy test, eyes still locked. They
break each other's gaze and look down at the test again.

Sofi takes a deep, relieved breath. She glances up at Ryan
and sees disappointment in his face. He was ready. He looks
at her and she instinctively looks away, ashamed.

                                        BACK TO:


INT. SUBURBAN HOUSE - DAY

Sofi is rattled by the memory and barely hanging in there.

                    MEL
            Turn all the way around.

One couple fails. Sofi and Ryan carefully spin in a circle,
eyes locked. They make it. Ryan's face lights up.

Sofi can't take any more. She backs away. The ball drops
between them. Ryan is confused.

                    MEL (O.S.) (CONT'D)
            You're out! We have a winner!

As the other couple celebrates, Sofi continues backing away.
She turns and exits the room.


INT. RYAN AND SOFI'S APARTMENT - DAY [FLASHBACK]

Sofi sets an envelope on the dining room table. She turns
away, picks up a moving box, and goes out the front door.

The ENVELOPE is addressed to "Ryan".

                                        BACK TO:


INT. JULIE'S RESTROOM - DAY

Sofi tries to process things. She looks in the mirror at
herself but immediately looks away ashamed...confused...

                    SOFI
                (to herself)
            Why are you so scared?
                (beat)
            What do you want?

She shakes her head, still unsure. A KNOCK at the door.

                    NIC (O.S.)
          Sof?

Sofi composes herself and opens the door to reveal Nic.

                    NIC (CONT'D)
               (worried)
          Are you ok?

                    SOFI
          I'm fine. I'm sorry for...
               (gesturing)
          ...everything.

Nic enters the bathroom with Sofi and closes the door.

                    NIC
          You didn't do anything. I'm sorry.
          I didn't think he'd come. You know
          how there's that person you're sure
          won't show but will probably still
          mail a gift, so you send them an
          invitation anyway? That was Ryan!
          Or so we thought.

                    SOFI
          It's not your fault. At all. I'm
          just...confused.

                    NIC
          Don't worry -- you'll figure it
          out. You always do. You're Sofi,
          and you're amazing. My hero.

Nic pulls her into a hug.

                    NIC (CONT'D)
          Wanna know a secret?

Sofi nods.

                    NIC (CONT'D)
               (touching her belly)
          We're naming her Sofia Rae. Sofi.

This hits Sofi hard. She touches Nic's belly too.

                    SOFI
          You're gonna be a great mother.

Nic smiles, moved.

INT. SUBURBAN HOUSE - DAY

Sofi rejoins everyone as Nic is opens gifts with her husband,
JOHN (30s), at her side. Sofi stays on the periphery.

Nic opens Sofi's gift and produces a onesie. Everyone "oohs"
and "ahs" at how cute it is. Nic shows John. She then shows
her belly, as if showing the baby.

                    NIC
              (to Sofi)
          Thank you!

She sets the onesie on a stack of other onesies.

The stack unnerves Sofi. She gave something typical, totally
unlike her.

She watches as Nic waits for Mel to hand her the next
present. Nic caresses her belly and whispers to it. She takes
John's hand. The ideal family.

Sofi smiles a sad smile. She looks over and sees Ryan
watching from the kitchen, alone. She considers him and then
moves around the back way to him.

She joins him to watch Nic. She works up the courage to say:

                    SOFI
              (serious)
          I'm sorry.

He knows she's not talking about the game.

                    RYAN
          It's ok. It was just a game.

                    SOFI
          No, not that.
              (beat)
          I wasn't ready.

Beat as he processes.

                    RYAN
          And you're still not?

She offers an apologetic smile.

                    RYAN (CONT'D)
          Sofi, I don't know if I'm going to
          be able to keep waiting for you.

> SOFI
> (delicately)
> I don't think you should.

He nods, disappointed but understanding. They watch Nic and her husband, who are huddled close and talking and laughing.


INT. SUBURBAN HOUSE - DAY

Sofi and Nic hug goodbye in the entryway.


EXT. SOFI'S APARTMENT - DAY

Sofi hurries towards her apartment door.


INT. SOFI'S APARTMENT - DAY

Sofi rushes in, drops her things, and enters her art studio. Paintings and art supplies are all over the place. She picks up a blank canvas.

She removes her sunglasses to reveal tear-streaked eyes that are dry now. There's a hint of inspiration in her eyes.


INT. SOFI'S APARTMENT - DAY

MONTAGE of Sofi painting, mixing more paint, and getting really into her art, obviously inspired.

We catch glimpses of it, but don't see it in full until...


INT. NIC'S NURSERY ROOM - DAY

SOFI'S PAINTING is on a wall -- a mother and child scene. Nic straightens it and then steps back to take a look at it. She smiles.


EXT. HOUSTON - DAY

Sofi sketches at an outdoor cafe table. Done, she packs up, rises and heads to the corner of the street in the heart of downtown Houston.

She stops and considers her direction. She walks away up Main Street with confidence in her step.

FADE OUT

# CAST

| | |
|---:|:---|
| SOFI | BLAIR AULT |
| NIC | AMY GRISBEE |
| LANA | LAURA HELMERS |
| MEL | LAUREN BONETTI |
| RYAN | JON MYLES |
| SEXY GUY IN BAR | DAVE MACKIE |
| WOMAN IN PARK | LISA FENLEY |
| CHILD IN PARK | CHLOE FENLEY |
| SHOWER ATTENDEES | LISA BODET |
| | R.T. BODET |
| | CHERIE BRIGHT |
| | RUDY BRIGHT |
| | BUDDY BROWN |
| | JEREMY GRISBEE |
| | JUSTIN HANCOCK |
| | CORISSA WANDMACHER |

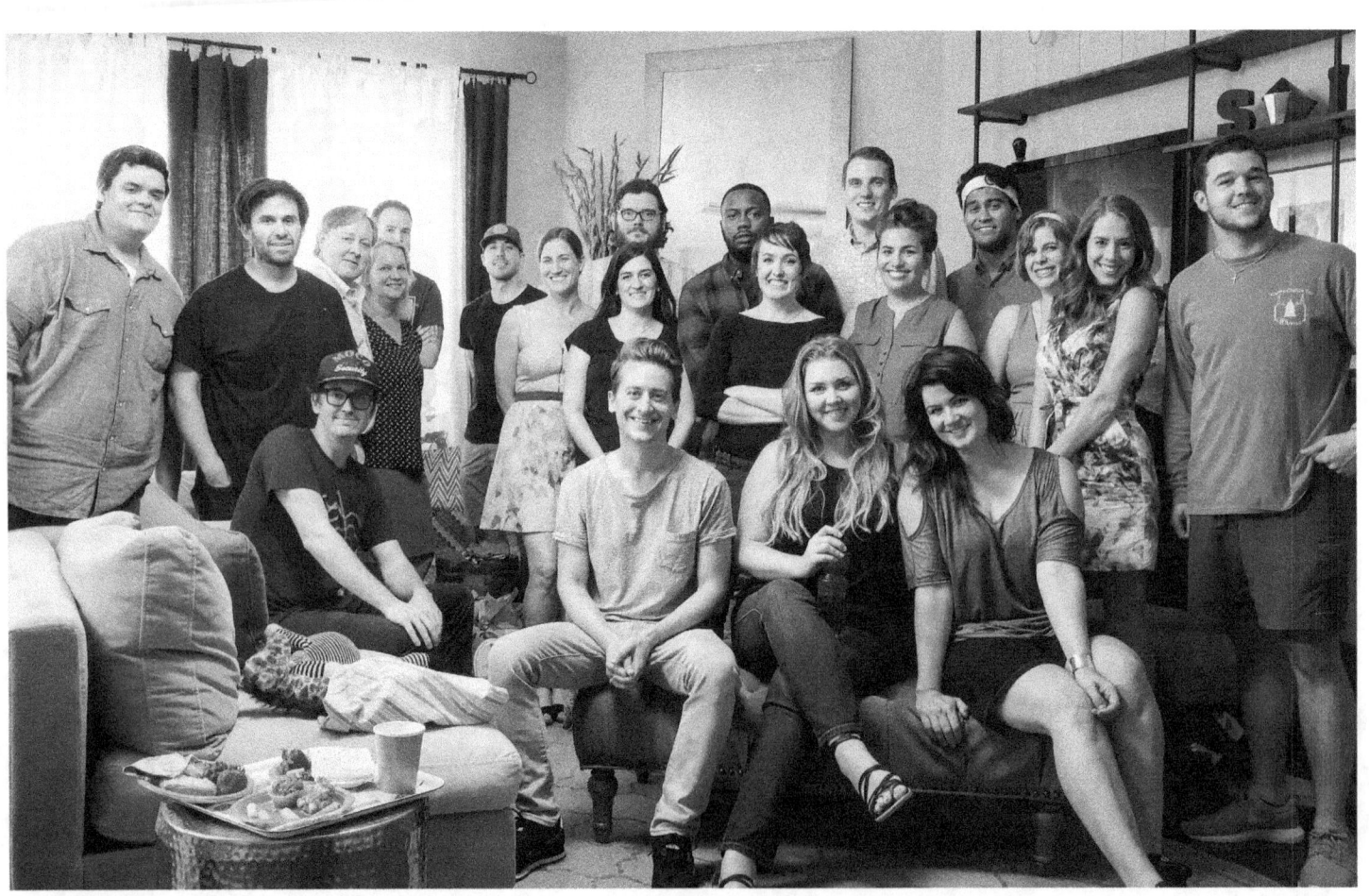

# CREW

| | |
|---|---|
| WRITER / DIRECTOR / EDITOR | NATHAN NIX |
| DIRECTOR OF PHOTOGRAPHY | JOEY MATHEWS |
| PRODUCTION DESIGNER | LIZ KILGORE |
| COMPOSER / PRODUCTION SOUND / SOUND MIXER | MICHAEL RAZMANDI |
| ORIGINAL ART BY | MEREDITH RICHEY |
| CAMERA OPERATORS | BRITTAN PITTMAN |
| | JOEY MATHEWS |
| MAKEUP ARTIST | CRYSTAL COOK |
| GRIPS | RYAN CLEMENTS |
| | TINA CORNELIUS |
| | ELYSSA RADENZ |
| | MICHAEL THOMAS |
| SCRIPT SUPERVISOR | ALEXANDER NOLAND |
| DRONE OPERATOR | RYAN CLEMENTS |
| EXECUTIVE PRODUCERS | KEN NIX |
| | PEGGY NIX |
| | NATHAN NIX |
| PRODUCERS | JOEY MATHEWS |
| | NATHAN NIX |
| ASSOCIATE PRODUCERS | JULIE BEDINGFIELD |
| | STEVEN BEDINGFIELD |
| | MORGAN GULLETT |
| | LAWRENCE LAMBON |
| | MICHAEL RAZMANDI |

# SPECIAL THANKS

KICKSTARTER SUPPORTERS

FILM LAB CREATIVE

THE HONEYMOON

POISON GIRL

HIGH SCHOOL FOR THE PERFORMING AND VISUAL ARTS

MELISSA BRUBAKER

LINDSAY MISTRETTA

ANGELA LEE

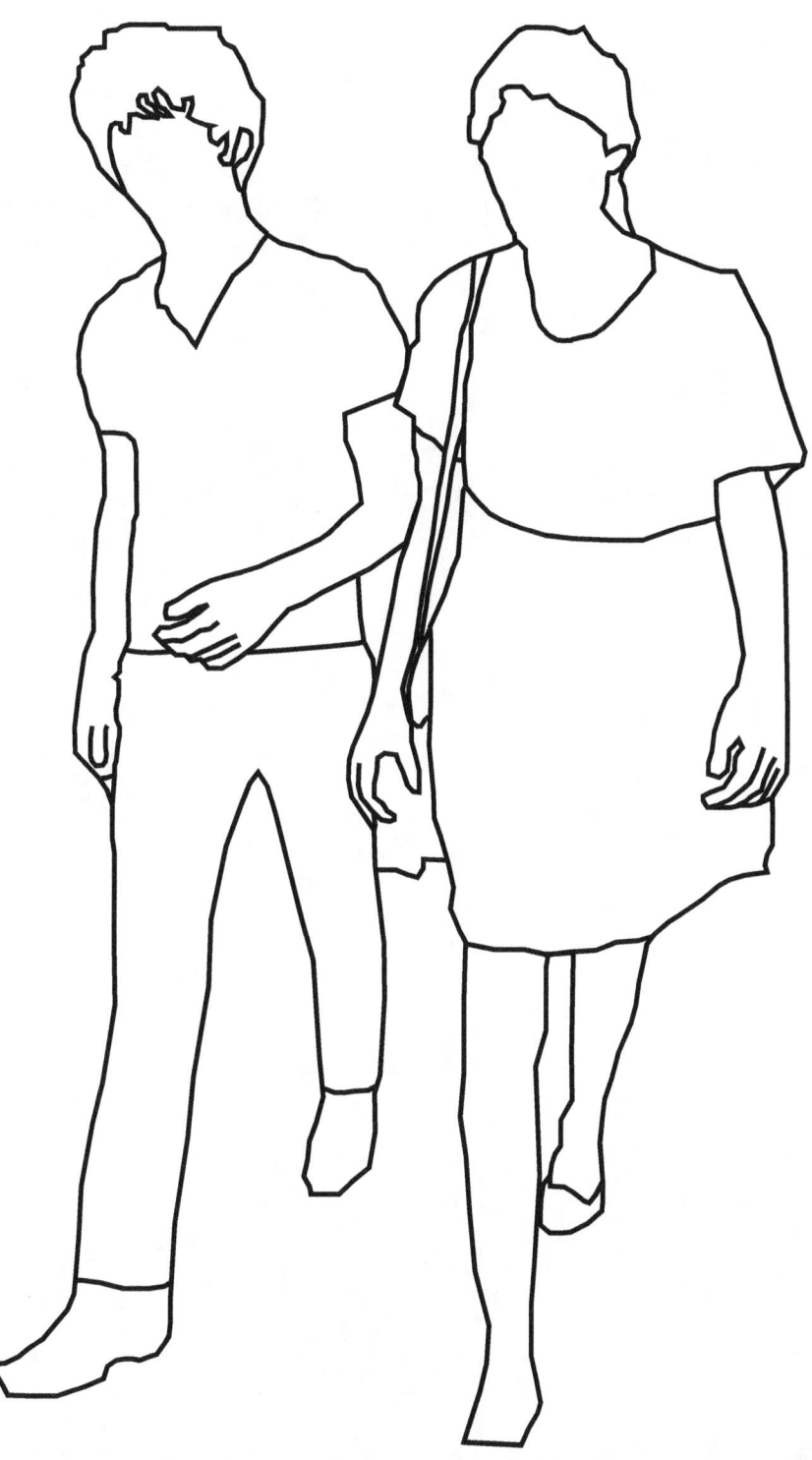

# EVERYBODY REPRODUCES

## A SHORT STORY BY NATHAN NIX

"I have a totally platonic favor to ask that involves alcohol and babies."

Sofi says this upon entering the restaurant's back office. The sentence falls out of her mouth like it was just another hum-drum element of her pre-shift ritual, as though the potentially life-changing favor carries no more weight than locking her purse up, strapping on the black apron, or straightening her tie and checking her crisp white dress shirt for wrinkles. It was something she felt unimportant enough to casually toss over her shoulder while she busied herself with the aforementioned necessary tasks.

Typically, the implications of the statement (If actually platonic and with sex truly ruled out, we're still looking at either a sinister practical joke or kidnapping—either way, jail time) would at least require a normal person to face you as they asked it, perhaps even looking you in the eye if they had the boldness. Again—with a normal person.

Sofi is not normal. She has a tendency to keep her Tupperware and china on the same shelf; and, likewise, on more than one occasion, she has used spur-of-the-moment decision-making processes in monumental situations.

"No way," I tell her.

She tries the whole "I helped you quit smoking, so you owe me" trick, but we both know the score on that one—she brought a box of Nicoderm to a White Elephant gift exchange and I happened to end up with it. And used it.

"You can look at is as me saving your life," she says, "which means you perpetually owe me a favor, since, you know, you wouldn't even be around if it weren't for me."

It's a move that's worked in the past, but I know how to counter it now.

"Your claim doesn't hold up—I haven't stopped smoking, so I don't owe you anything."

It's a bittersweet win, I guess. Battle won, war lost.

"*What?*"

"Yeah, I kinda started up again."

"Why?"

"Because…I don't know…"

Because smoking distracts me, and distraction is my nicotine these days as life meanders along.

"How can you even ask me why I'm still smoking?" I say. "You still smoke. Until you stop, you've got nothing to say to me."

"Well, despite your ungratefulness, I'm gonna attempt to save your life once more. You smoking again is just another reason you should be my date to this 'couples' baby shower' being thrown for Lana and Aiden in Spring. There'll be lots of kids running around, so you won't be able to smoke anywhere—not without getting the stink eye from every mom there."

"Let's back up a second…two seconds, actually. First, Aiden and Lana had the gall to reproduce again?"

"Ha!"

It's a genuine gut-bust laugh—the kind you can't keep down because what was said rings so true that it hits your core like a lumberjack slamming a mallet onto the pivot of the boardwalk game Ring the Bell. The laugh just shoots up and bursts out.

Through the frosted glass of the office windows, I can make out the silhouettes of the customers dining nearest the office as they turn and look our way, searching for the source of the joyous bark that interrupted their candle-lit Italian meal.

"Hey, keep it down," I chide.

"But it's *so* true! What the hell were they thinking? Don't they understand the inevitable perversion they're releasing on society? They're breeding future date rapists."

"Damn masochists is what they are," I say. "Instead of a name bracelet, the hospital might as well get a security guard to clamp on a GPS ankle tracker and alert the probation officer. *But anyway,* secondly, you said it was a 'couples' baby shower?"

"Yes, I did," she says, wiping the tears born of laughter from her eyes and settling back down.

"But we're not a couple."

"We used to be a couple."

"Well, according to your past arguments, that was never the case."

"Well, we used to sleep together," she counters.

"That didn't make us a couple—it just made us confused and awkward around each other… made *me* confused and awkward, you cold, cold…"

"Aw," she says, thrusting out her lower lip as she pulls the bow tight behind her apron. She rounds the desk and sits on the side of my rolling chair before putting an arm around me, leaning in close, and squeezing me against her like she's comforting a little brother with a scraped knee. "But it also made us best friends, right?"

"God knows how."

"And best friends who used to sleep together have to pretend to be a couple from time to time so all their old friends from high school, who are now married with kids or gay, don't think they're losers or gay, openly pity them, and offer to set them up with other singles who really are losers."

"Or gay."

"Yup, or gay."

"*Or,*" I counter, "best friends who used to sleep together and are now single and approaching thirty could just not go to places where they could be misconstrued as losers. Or gay."

"Like the suburbs?" she asks.

"Exactly."

"You can get mistaken for being a loser or gay here in The Montrose," she says.

"But nobody gives a shit in The Montrose, because everybody here *is* a loser or gay."

"And that's why we love it," she says. "You can't be scared of going home, though. Plus I already told Lana we were coming, so we're committed."

"In other words, there was no way you could get out of it, so you're dragging me down with you."

"Yup. Dragging you *home* with me."

"Just like old times."

+++

I hadn't seen Sofi so attached to a permanent marker since fifth grade, when she used to hold it under her nose while we waited at the bus stop (and on the bus…and down the school hallway… and pretty much until Mrs. Ulrich snatched it away in study hall, leaving her with a streak of black on her nostril and the promise to return it at the end of the day). It had only been in her possession for two or three minutes tops when yet another fifth grade teacher snatched it out of

Sofi's hand, which was dangling with apathy at her side. The thief fast-walked away, a throaty cackle drifting back over her shoulder in her wake. It took five seconds of bewilderment for Sofi to conjure the appropriate response.

No, wait. I conjured the *appropriate* response. Sofi stuck with the study hall refrain.

"That bitch!"

Despite being nearly two decades on from elementary school, she still mumbled it under her breath.

"What?" I whispered. "It's just a marker. You didn't want it anyway."

"If she would've just asked, I'd have given it to her," Sofi replied, training a stink-eye of her own on the lady, who was in the living room raising the spoils above her head for all to see and thus congratulate her on her subversion.

"Now, though, it's *on*. My only goal today is to get that marker back."

"What about preserving your sense of accomplishment in life?"

"Who cares? That bitch stole my marker. I'm gonna make her pay."

And she probably will, but almost definitely not in a proportionate manner.

When Lana had invited us into the house, her best friend had attempted to hand us the markers and an explanation. Sofi and I tried to decline both politely, insisting we weren't the games type, but were instead the wallflowers necessary to fill the quorum.

Candi, "with an i and not a y," as she proudly informed us (which immediately piqued our collective interest, as it provided the potential that she was more than simply another teacher, but might also moonlight as a stripper), told us, "everybody has to play, y'all!"

"No, really, it's ok," I insisted, the sentence losing momentum as she dropped a marker into the front pocket of my lightweight pearl-snap button-up.

Sofi didn't have a front pocket, but she had cleavage, something she made sure of before we left—she may not have kids yet, but at least her boobs were still at their original height. She could hold onto that (as have many a man).

When Sofi refused to put her hand out for the marker, Candi spent a moment waving it around in front of her, as though the teacher/stripper was also an instructor at Hogwart's. Exactly one second after Candi realized the marker would rest comfortably in the natural nook between Sofi's breasts, Sofi realized the inexcusably friendly teacher/stripper/witch might actually drop it there.

The former wallflower accepted the baton, entering us in a competition equally as silly and entertaining as watching pencil-thin freaks of nature wearing short shorts and oversized numbers sprint in an oval pattern around an inexplicably long running track.

The rules of the game were simple: collect as many markers as you could. The person with the most would win a prize. You could obviously steal markers, but, as the day went on, we discovered you could also barter for them, cajole the smaller of the group, employ people's kids as double-agents, and even parlay former high school glory into residual dominance, taking advantage of still-low self-esteem.

Well, other people could. Sofi was immediately handicapped by three middle school years of smoking cigarettes with long-haired kids in Pantera t-shirts behind the 7-11, four high school years of smoking pot behind the gym with the kids in rap-rock bands, and a lifetime of art classes and paintings that "peeled back the façade of who we want people to think we are" to reveal "the ordinary beauty at our core."

After that juried show in our Junior year, with "the Incident" where Sofi took the hypocrisy she witnessed among her fellow students as the major inspiration for her blue ribbon collection, everyone was inherently suspicious of her at any and all times. They all knew that when she watched and listened to a conversation, she *watched* and *listened* to the conversation, noting and analyzing, and, eventually, interpreting. When she came around, markers, handbags, and dignity were clutched tightly to partygoers chests.

I would have had no problem with someone stealing my marker and taking away the subconscious pressure of having to guard it, but, for some reason, nobody bothered to snatch it. Actually, one person did, but only jokingly. She quickly returned it, accompanied by a laugh, saying, "I'm just kidding. I couldn't do that to you."

Sentiments like that were peppered into many conversations I had over the course of the party, and it fueled my theory that everyone there knew all the details of everyone else's personal life, even if they feigned ignorance. The need to make sure Ryan's marker stayed in his breast pocket, keeping his heart company, probably stemmed from the presence of Nic—short for Nicole—my ex-girlfriend.

Everyone knew her—she was nominated for Homecoming Queen and Miss Woodlands back in high school—and everyone knew me through her. Better said, everyone *talked* to me because of her. They already knew me—even though I was a few years older than most of them—because I was the nicest of the upperclassman smoking under the bleachers every day in high school. Even still, they never talked to me then unless they wanted to bum-and-run, which was a source of great entertainment for us outsiders. The greatest fun was had when we lied about having a lighter on us, forcing them to light off the cig we were smoking. Why was it fun? We never took the cig out of our mouth while they were lighting, playing on their fear of getting within twelve inches of us. Our cigarettes were good enough for them, but we might as well have been lepers.

I was granted talkable status when Nic and I fell for each other and started dating during her first year at community college. That was at the genesis of her "drift," as she likes to refer to the shifting of friends and interests she underwent as a result of not being able to go to UT-Austin with her cheerleader and jock friends, and having to slum it at Montgomery Community College with me, Sofi, Aiden, and her own friend, Lana. It took awhile for her old friends to realize I hadn't cast a degenerate spell on her, and that her transformation truly was genuine and thought-out. When they came to terms with her new interest in art and dive bars and music they'd never heard of, they were finally able to see me as more than a catalyst of grime. Nonetheless, they still felt it necessary to punish me with greasy, Counting Crows and Gin Blossoms-soundtracked double dates at chain restaurants, all under the pretense of "bonding."

Then she left me.

Not only me, but the whole damn country. Did the whole backpacking around Europe thing, then settled in London for a while, working for an art gallery.

I never understood why she left. I was already at my lowest point, and I needed her to be there. But she took off.

And now she's back. Apparently. I point this out to Sofi.

"She's back. Apparently."

"Yeah…" Sofi replies, dragging the word out as she probably figures out what to tack onto it.

"You don't seem surprised," I say.

"Yeah…"

"Because you already knew," I say, filling in all the things I can tell she can't figure out how to admit to me.

"Yeah."

It doesn't drag out like the others, because it's a confession.

"Did you know she'd be here?" I ask.

"No. She told me she was gonna be out of town. Come on—I'd never do that to you."

I know she wouldn't, too, so I can't be upset with her.

"Well, at least she's alone," I mutter. "I'd totally split if she was here with some new guy. Hey, if she came alone, you could've come alone, too."

"Yeah…" she says, letting it drag out again. I just shake my head as her lips curl in a devious smile.

+++

I manage to avoid being in the same room as Nic for a good half hour, though it costs me being able to avoid *other* conversations I didn't want to have, like the one where all the guys grab a beer and head into the garage.

Honestly, the guys gathered in the garage thing was something I didn't expect—not at Aiden's house. At the house of any other guy present, yeah; but all one would ever really find in Aiden's garage in years past was a drum set and posters of Victoria's Secret models.

Times had changed though. His garage was now like the garages of any of the guys we'd never have hung out with back in the day. They were the garages of our dads—tools, workbenches, hunting equipment, and the subject of our visit, his latest All-Terrain Vehicle. It was called The BOB, and it was a stroller. Not just any stroller though; it was an SUS—a Sport Utility Stroller.

"It's a beaut," says the night manager at Gander Mtn., himself a stroller aficionado as the father of three kids, the oldest of which is 11. Gander Mtn. guy is a year younger than me.

"What are those wheels—12 inches?" he inquires.

"Yup," Aiden says as we all stand around it, beers in hand. "Five-point padded harness, too. State of the art suspension. Bought the weather shield to go with it," he adds, nodding over at a gargantuan piece of plastic that resembles a HazMat mask. The BOB and shield seem a terrific combination for showing your kid the eye of a Category 4.

"Whole thing set me back four bills," Aiden states proudly.

"Damn, man," I say. "That's a helluva investment in child transportation."

"Yup. Had to sell the drums to free up the cash for it."

I turn, eyebrows raised. The drums were complete trash, but Aiden had always refused to upgrade from them, even when his parents offered to front him the money. He'd learned everything he knew about percussion on them, and I wouldn't be surprised if there had developed some masochistic attachment between drummer/punisher and kit/slave.

"You take it down to the creek yet?" asks the other guy present, who manages a local DirecTV installation crew. With Aiden managing a Discount Tire location, all four of us had somehow ended up in positions of minor authority, stumbling ass-first into them as we killed time waiting for something to happen after dropping out of college. Everyone but me had figured they might as well start having kids. That's what you do, right?

"Naw, not yet," Aiden replies. "I'm gonna though. Gotta wait for a day when Lana's out of town, just in case things get too messy to clean up in an hour."

I don't know if he's talking about the stroller getting too messy or the kid. He sighs a satisfied sigh.

"Yup, never before in my life have I wanted to take my kid through so much rough terrain."

"Gotta get 'em hooked young," Gander Mtn. guy says, the other guys murmuring their agreement. Gander Mtn. guy then asks the question he's been waiting to pop since he first set eyes on The BOB.

"Mind if I take it for a spin?"

+++

A half-hour later, it's game time inside. *Couples'* game time. Fortunately, adult refreshments are involved, though we're down one vodka-filled watermelon (no moms—especially not his wife—would allow Gander Mtn. guy to take any of their kids for a "spin" in The BOB, which proved to be a shrewd move, considering the vivid image of a watermelon splattered across the driveway after he lost control of the SUS on a flower bed jump. An *awesome* flower bed jump.).

The girls are already seated in the living room, gossiping in bunches as the guys enter and join their respective partner. Sofi, Nic, and Lana have taken up residence on the main couch.

Nic looks healthy and stylish, yet she is void of the pretense one would expect from spending so much time in Europe. She is pure loveliness, having left a confused young girl and returned a woman. Her abandonment of me still smolders though, and the joy of seeing her is mixed with the lingering resentment of having been deemed unwanted at best or corrosive at worst. I suddenly feel underdressed. Not just underdressed but also underwhelming. When I first met her, I was the streetwise sage, showing her the possibilities of the world. For a while after, I could feel myself stagnating under the strain of the realities of that same world, while she adapted and grew to the point where we were equals. Now she seems to have matured and left me in regression.

She speaks with assurance, as though she's lived an entire life and discovered the secret of contentment in her journeys. This secret was shown to her by glamorous foreign lovers, of course. And now she's returned, either broke as shit or full of so much wisdom that she's learned to make peace with being in this city, with these people, all of which she used to feel repressed her. My guess would be she's not broke as shit.

In other words, it's the exact opposite of when Sofi moved to New York City to break into the painting world and returned with her tail between her legs, angry at herself for not being able to cut it.

Despite Nic's confidence, she glances up and around the room regularly enough that I know Sofi told her I was at the party. Just knowing I'm still able to have that affect on her—or any affect, really—encourages me. Enough so, in fact, that I finally step out of hiding and move toward them.

When I approach, Lana attempts to rise.

"No, don't get up—you're cool where you are," I insist, raising my voice a bit to be heard above the chatter and commotion around us. "I'll stand."

"Nah, you gotta sit with your lady for the games," she says, shifting one labored breath at a time into position to hoist herself up off the couch. "And there's no way we're getting a fourth on this thing—not with my fat ass taking up half of it. My beautiful, skinny girls over here are already practically sitting on top of each other. But that's ok, 'cause they're so light anyway. Everyone's stayed so skinny. It's wonderful. Just wonderful."

Aiden comes over, helps pull her up, and then leads her over to a large recliner. She settles into her throne as he stands next to her. He then leans on the back of the recliner, which slowly pushes it down and in a clockwise motion.

"Baby, don't do that," Lana says without looking at him.

"Oh, right—sorry," he says, standing up straight, but not leaving his spot next to his woman. I've never seen him so obliging in his life.

I give Nic an awkward smile as I sit one over from her on the couch, Sofi in the middle.

"Hey," I say.

"Hey there. How are you?" she asks.

"Good, good. And you?"

"Good."

"Great," I say.

Just great.

I'm gonna need another drink for this.

Candi hops up and claps her hands and talks at the same time, trying to get our attention as though we were a room full of her little wizards and witches.

"All right, y'all—it's game time!"

A few "woo!"s go up from some of the girls.

"I'm gonna need another drink for this," Sofi says to Nic and I as she leans back into the couch. "Does anyone else find it ironic that the one person who could really do with getting hammered right now is the only one who can't?" she asks, nodding our attention toward Lana.

Sofi downs the rest of her beverage, and it's only then I notice she's been holding and drinking from a sippy cup.

"Really?" I ask, nodding toward it.

"I saw it sitting in the dish strainer earlier," she explains. "I've always wanted to try one, so I mixed my Jack and Coke in it instead of the disposable plastic cups. Honestly, if I ran a bar, I'd insist every drink was served in one of these. They're perfect for drunks, who act like children anyway." She holds it out by one of the handles, shakes it around, and turns it upside down, the ice inside rattling.

I shake my head.

"It got a big laugh when I came back into the living room earlier," she says. "Don't be jealous."

"I'm not jealous."

"You will be when you go home with a stain on the front of your shirt, and I go home clean as a whistle," she replies, giving me a wink.

"Apparently, 'clean' is a relative term," Nic quips, breaking her reservation and smiling at Sofi and I.

"Seriously?" Sofi asks. "You're gonna give me shit too?"

I chuckle.

"Now you take his side," Sofi jokes.

Nic blushes and Sofi realizes her error.

"I didn't mean it like that," she says, appealing to each of us. "Sorry."

"It's ok," Nic says.

"We're gonna play the 'dirty' diaper game first," Candi says, picking up a tray filled with diapers that have been soiled with melted chocolate bars.

"Whoa, buddy," Sofi says, leaning forward. "I'm gonna get that drink *right now*."

She eases off the couch and high-tails it toward the kitchen.

"Where are you going?" Candi asks after her, but Sofi ignores the question and disappears down a hallway. "Where's she going?" Candi then asks Nic and I as she continues to pass out the diapers.

"I don't know. She saw the diapers and suddenly started muttering about kids and a pool," I say.

"I thought she didn't have kids," Candi says.

I shrug and bite my lower lip. Candi returns my shrug and moves on with her tray. Nic had been leaning forward, legs crossed, elbow on knee, arm straight up, and her palm cupping her chin. She's since allowed her head to tilt down so her palm covers her mouth. Her tiny hands aren't big enough to hide the edges of her smile though.

I instinctively smile back, which prompts her to shake her head slightly.

"You're terrible," she mutters into her hand.

"You know you like it," I respond.

Candi leads everyone through the diaper game, where we have to taste the melted chocolate and try to guess which candy bar it is. Some have nuts. That's all I'm saying about that.

We then play a similar game where we have to taste unlabeled baby food and try to guess the flavor.

Sofi has yet to resurface, so the only thing filling the distance between Nic and I are the occasional instinctive knowing glances one shares with an old friend. As the games progress and the glances continue, I think we both feel alternately guilty and warmed by their reoccurring nature.

"All right, everyone on their feet," Candi says, yet again clapping her hands. My reluctance to rise brings back memories of fifth grade Ryan, on the cusp of adolescence and too cool to be caught willingly participating in organized fun. I think fifth grade Ryan was on to something.

Then a realization about Candi fills my mind that is so adult in nature, I'm somewhat ashamed to admit it hatched in my conscience. It dons on me that her enthusiasm and knack for directing activities and keeping everyone focused and involved would be commendable if she were *my* child's teacher.

I look over at Nic, and she smiles back, causing me to look away quickly. Everything is reactive. I don't know what the hell is going on, and I can't corral my actions or thoughts.

"What?" Nic asks.

"What? What what?" I reply, trying to shake off this thing.

"Oh, I thought…" she says, stopping short, confused. "Nothing. Nevermind."

The room is quiet, and Nic and I notice Candi staring at us, waiting patiently for us to stop talking.

"Ok, then," she says, "we're going to play Tennis Ball Trouble. Grab your partner and make

34

some room for yourself."

Sofi still hasn't returned. I know she hasn't left because I drove, so she has to either be outside smoking and talking on her phone, or upstairs playing Wii with the kids. I see her absence as an excuse to decamp to the kitchen and fix myself a drink before seeking her out, but Candi catches me as my knee bends to take the first step.

"Where are you going?"

"Um, well…my partner seems to have disappeared, so I'm gonna go see if I can find her," I say.

"The game'll be over by the time you return," she says, seeming genuinely worried that I'll miss the satisfaction this particular game can bring to a person. "No, we can't have that," she continues. "You know Nicole, right? Well, she doesn't have a partner either, so you two can be each other's partner."

"Oh, uh…um…" Nic stutters.

"Good—it's settled then," Candi says, turning away to make sure everyone else is partnered up.

Nic and I look at each other and force smiles, the awkwardness of earlier suddenly having crept back in.

"So, we're partners again," she says.

"Yeah, guess so."

"Well, as long as I don't have to hum *Supercalifragilisticexpialidocious* for you to guess, I think we'll be ok," she says, referring to the disastrous way a game of Cranium ended the night we first hung out and got to know each other.

"Yeah, for real," I reply. Thoughts and questions and theories fill my mind, breaking up any substantive response to continue the chitchat.

"So, um, how you been?" I ask. She opens her mouth to respond, but it closes again when Candi steps up and hands me a tennis ball.

"Here's what you do…" Candi says to everyone. "Guys—take the tennis ball and hold it against your forehead like this," she instructs, demonstrating. I obey. "Now…ladies, step forward and press your forehead against the other side of the tennis ball, so the ball is wedged between each of your foreheads."

I must be quite a sight with a tennis ball pressed against my forehead and my mouth dropped open, which it does when it hits me just how uncomfortable this game is about to get, literally and figuratively. Nic takes a deep breath and looks at all the other couples as they bend down and adjust to make their foreheads meet just right. They're all laughing and dropping the ball and bickering about who does what to make the ball stay—"No, you lean forward, and *I'll* stand still." "No, baby, it's not gonna work unless we both lean into each other."

I've been standing for too long by myself with this stupid tennis ball held against my forehead, so I motion her toward me.

"Come here," I say. She approaches, and I lean down to line up my forehead with hers.

"I never thought I'd stoop to your level," I say, and she shakes her head at the bad joke. It brings a brief smile back though.

Then fucking Candi takes forever explaining the simplest instructions, forcing Nic and I to stand leaning against each other, a tennis ball apart, nowhere else to look but into the other person's eyes, nothing else to smell but the other's breath and cologne or perfume (the same perfume that turns my head in every department store *every* damn time to this day), nothing else to do except try to focus on what Candi's saying while warding off all the memories of what it felt like when our heart rates rose every time we got this close and time stood still and everything seemed possible and probable and just perfect.

In her intent eyes, I see yearning for what could have been—what *should* have been. I also see fear. It's the fear of what might have been, what might still be. It's the same fear I saw one night, a month before she left, when she sat across from me on her bed, waiting, shaking the pregnancy test, and waiting some more. When she realized nothing had shown up yet, positive or negative, her eyes had focused on mine again, searching them out and finding nothing to comfort her.

I was ready that night. My heart was in my throat, and I did everything in my power to will a positive result. She had cried when it finally showed up negative, and I think I shed a tear too. We cried for different reasons. Hers was relief and fear of what came next. Of what could come next.

Perhaps we didn't cry for different reasons, then, because my tears were also out of fear of what would come next. I could already feel her pulling away.

And now life had brought us back together, distanced only by a furry yellow round thing.

The goal, of course, was to keep the ball from dropping. Candi barked out directions, and each couple moved left together, then right, then down, up, left quicker, right quicker, a hop, a full turn, and, finally, a lowering all the way to the ground—on our bellies—and back up again.

Nic and I made it all the way through the hop, which we were surprised we pulled off. Instinctively, wide eyes and wider smiles stretched across our faces. Moments later, though, Nic pulls away unexpectedly halfway through the full turn. I thought we were going to make it—the chemistry was just right and the adrenaline was flowing—but she backs off and the tennis ball drops onto the carpet, barely bouncing.

"Damn," she says.

"We almost had it," I say, confused. "What happened?"

"I think our balance was off," she replies.

"It didn't feel to me like our balance was off."

She bites her bottom lip and shrugs.

"You're out of the game!" Candi yells, pointing at us.

+++

A stream of kids flood down the stairs, through the living room (to kiss mommy and daddy), and out the door to the backyard, and Nic and I use the commotion to slip in with them and head outside.

I follow her as she walks to the edge of the patio and stops, all the kids leaving us behind as they converge on the jungle gym. She looks to the left side of the backyard and squints into the late-afternoon Texas sun. A breeze blows, and she takes it in with a big, reinvigorating breath. She closes her eyes and smiles.

Her hair flutters backward, and for a moment she is the golden Texas goddess I knew she had been before she met me.

A straggler with dark hair passes me and approaches Nic from behind. He creeps up and swings his little arm at her butt. His palm slaps the cheek as hard as a five-year-old can, which is hard enough to make Nic yelp and swivel around, her eyes narrowed and brow furrowed as she locates the source.

"Nice ass, baby!" the kid yells with a lisp before throwing his head back, giggling, and running out to join the rest of the group.

"That little jackass," she says, astonished. "Can you believe he just did that?"

"Well…yeah, actually. That's Aiden and Lana's kid. Or, to pinpoint responsibility even more, that's *Aiden's son.*"

"Holy crap, I haven't seen him since he was a baby. I didn't even recognize him."

We each take a seat on patio chairs, and for a few seconds, I allow myself the false notion that this is our patio, our backyard, and that one of the kids out there is also ours.

If Aiden and Lana's kid turned out the way he did, what would our kid have turned out like? Polite and graceful like its mother? Shy like its dad? Would it have had her bright eyes and cheerleader smile, or would it have had my dark, suspicious gaze and devious half-grin?

Would it treat people with respect and patience, or would it go wherever its heart led it, regardless of other people's feelings?

What physical and character traits would get reproduced, and what would it fight against inheriting?

The back door opens, and Sofi flutters out, her eyes scanning the jungle gym. She doesn't even see us.

"Hey," Nic says, "where have you been?"

Sofi jerks her head our way, and her wide eyes swallow us for a second before spitting us back out and refocusing on the kids.

"No time to explain. I've gotta…"

Her words trail off as she steps onto the grass and arrows toward the closest toddler. When she reaches him, she talks in a voice too low for Nic and I to make out. The kid stares blankly at her. She reaches down, gently takes his sippy cup out of his hands, and holds it up to her nose. With a shake of the head, she returns it to the kid, who waddles off toward the slide.

"Hey!" she says to a toddler waiting his turn to slide down. "Um…Colby. No…Connor. No. Crap. What was your name? Casey! Come here, Casey!"

Like the first kid, this one simply stares at her. She moves to the edge of the bridge running between the two wooden towers and reaches up, motioning for the toddler to come to her.

"Come here, buddy. Give me two seconds of your time."

The kid isn't budging. Sofi turns to her right and climbs the stepladder into the tower opposite Casey. Being a foot too tall for the tower, Sofi has to stay crouched when she reaches the top. With both hands, she picks up a little girl and moves her out of the way so she can cross the bridge. The girl's face puckers and a low bay ensues. Sofi ignores it and wobbles across the wooden planks, nearly losing her balance at the midpoint.

She reaches Casey just as he's about to go down the slide, and she grabs the tail of his tiny Skittle-green polo and pulls him back to her. He's perplexed. When Sofi yanks his sippy cup out of his hands, the sheer injustice of it all becomes too much for his little heart to take, and he cries close to a fifth interval above his future princess in the opposite tower, the two wailing in harmony.

"What on earth is going on out here?"

It's the fifth grade teacher. She uncrosses her arms, a batch of markers clenched tight in her right hand. She shifts them to the left as she steps out on the grass and strides toward the tower where Sofi is bent over, sippy cup in hand, a spooked look in her eyes.

"What are you doing to my kid?" she demands.

THE END

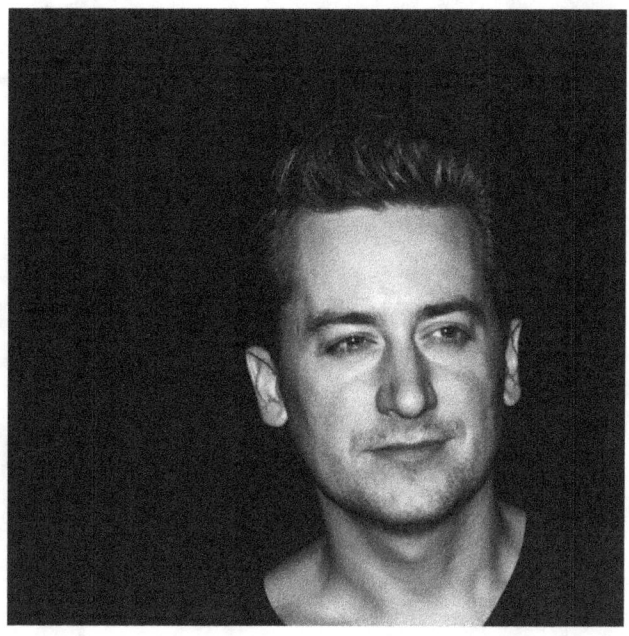

Nathan Nix (www.nathannix.com) studied journalism at the University of Houston. After graduating, he discovered he enjoyed making stories up from scratch more than working a reporter's beat. Given that most respectable publications tend to avoid fabrication, Nathan turned to fiction as a way to dodge a life of crime. In 2013, his Young Adult novel, *The Drifters*, was released. He is also the author of *Nathan's Tour of Houston: A Coloring Book*. His work has been featured on Relevant Magazine's website and in *Free Press Houston*, among other publications. *Sofi* is one of many screenplays he's written, and it's the basis for his second short film of the same name. He can be reached at nathan@nathannix. com. He'd love to hear from you. Really.

www.ingramcontent.com/pod-product-compliance
Lightning Source LLC
Chambersburg PA
CBHW081023170526
45158CB00010B/3138